UNIVERSITIES IN AMERICA.

An Inaugural Address

DELIVERED IN ANN ARBOR, MICHIGAN,

October 1st, 1863.

BY REV. E. O. HAVEN, D. D., LL. D.
PRESIDENT OF THE UNIVERSITY OF MICHIGAN.

PUBLISHED BY THE UNIVERSITY.

ANN ARBOR:
C. G. CLARK, JR., BOOK AND JOB PRINTER,
COURIER OFFICE.
1863.

ADDRESS.

[PREFATORY NOTE.—On Thursday, October 1st, 1863, the beginning of a College year for the University of Michigan, Rev. Dr. Haven was inaugurated as President of the University, in the morning, in the Presbyterian Church in Ann Arbor. In the afternoon the new Law Building was opened with appropriate exercises held in the Law Lecture Room. These exercises consisted of Prayer offered by Rev. Dr. Hogarth of Detroit, a Dedicatory Address by Prof. Thomas M. Cooley, and a Poem by D. Bethune Duffield, Esq., of Detroit. In the evening addresses were given in the Presbyterian Church by Rev. Lucius D. Chapin, A. M., Professor of Moral and Intellectual Philosophy, and Samuel G. Armor, M. D., Professor of Institutes of Medicine and Materia Medica.

The Inaugural Exercises consisted of Prayer by Rev. Mr. Inglis of Detroit, an Introductory Address by Hon. Donald McIntyre of Ann Arbor, in behalf of the Board of Regents, and the following Inaugural Address:]

GENTLEMEN OF THE BOARD OF REGENTS:

I am impressed with the conviction that the office to which you have called me demands all the thought and energy and industry of which I am capable. Whatever I may succeed in accomplishing, there will still be a vast area suggested to the imagination, of what will appear possible and desirable. I enter upon these duties with a deep sense of the necessity of the hearty co-operation of all who are interested in the management of the University, and with a profound feeling of dependence upon the approval and blessing of Almighty God.

The University of Michigan has not, like some institutions of the kind in other countries, a history of a thousand years, with usages that seem to rival in regularity the laws of nature. Such universities it must be comparatively easy to manage, for the machinery has moved so long and regularly as to seem almost to have acquired the power of spontaneous action. The ambition of their wisest friends is, therefore, to reform abuses, to remove incumbrances, to introduce new elements of efficiency, and to adjust the enginery to modern times.

"University Reform" is for this reason a common term in the older countries. But here everything is young. We have no moss-covered buildings poorly adapted to present use; no perverted patrimonies entailed to perpetuate usages that have lost their significance or are defunct; no ceremonies that have ceased to be significant; no sinecures occupied by men who observe the letter and violate the spirit of the law; no recognition of caste, exalting the undeserving and rejecting the worthy; no trammels upon the conscience; nor any other relics of the dark ages of Europe. Our difficulties are those which beset the early days of an enterprise. We have not yet passed out of the age of exuberant hopefulness, when rash experimentation often leads to waste of energy. Our greatest danger is dissatisfaction with the present and an impulsive determination to change what experience has proved to be useful and wise.

The University of Michigan is only about twenty years old. Many of those far-seeing and patriotic men who projected it and watched over its infant growth, and to whose commanding position and influence in public affairs its existence is due, are still with us, wearing the well-won honors of a patriotic and Christian life. Some of its earliest instructors still honor and strengthen the Faculty by their presence and labors. These first friends of the University are permitted to see, on the foundation which their own hands have laid, a majestic fabric arise, whose proportions I believe will yet expand into a temple, more majestic even than their imaginations ever conceived. In spite of difficulties, and revocations of plans, and disappointments—no greater, however, than might be expected, in so complicated and so novel an enterprise—the University of Michigan stands before the world to-day, a vital proof that a State University can prosper and be made to accomplish all that an intelligent community can demand of such an Institution.

In reviewing the brief history of this University we find

much to commend, and no great errors the exposure of which is needful for our future guidance. The mistakes that have been made are not such as would be likely to be repeated. Its first professors were men who had been educated in the older American colleges, who wisely adopted a course of study and instruction which accorded with the commonly received views of their time and country, and which American experience had ascertained to be the best adapted to meet the necessities of our youth. The first Faculty of the College of Science, Literature, and the Arts, were wise in establishing a high standard of scholarship as a requisite to graduation, which gave this University, at the first, a fair reputation among the oldest and best colleges of the country. This reputation it has always maintained.

Great credit is due to those who managed the affairs of this University during its early history, though for some reason an impression has prevailed among those unacquainted with the facts, that the University was not so conducted for several years as to meet the anticipation of its founders or the proper demands of the State. This impression is wrong.

It is true that for a time the University was embarrassed by local rivalries and a jealousy of centralization, and an honest though impracticable effort to divide it into branches, which, if it had been persisted in, would have substituted several high schools for one strong University; yet, in spite of these jealousies and differences of opinion, and in spite of the fearful monetary revolution which swept over the State and threatened to engulf all the property of the University, its course from the first was highly honorable and successful. All honor to the noble pioneers of this State, who, like the Pilgrims of New England, had scarcely set foot upon the soil and erected their humble dwellings and houses of worship, before they directed their attention to schools and a University. And honor too to the first Regents and Faculty, whose plans were so wisely laid and so carefully commenced, that all who have followed them have largely entered into their labors and enjoyed the fruit of their energy and sagacity. The first classes that graduated from this University were large in proportion to the population of this part of the country—pioneers though they were—and they were well educated men, and have furnished as large a proportion of eminently useful men as the alumni of any American college. In this respect, at least, the University of Michigan has been uniformly successful. The difficulties of its early history—such as they were—arose mostly from a want of money, for it is as impossible for a University to be strong and steadfast without an adequate material foundation, as for a soul to exist in this world without a body.

For the past ten years, with the rapid increase of the State of Michigan and the surrounding States, in population and wealth, the University has naturally increased. Its Faculties have increased, and its workings have been reduced to a system. Its Professors have become widely known as eminent in their respective professions. Its alumni have enlarged its influence and attractiveness. By the just generosity of the State the University has been relieved from the pressure of an enormous claim against it—which it would seem, however, from the records, it had already more than paid,—and has thus more than doubled its efficiency, and has received other tokens of material aid, that has increased the pabulum of its life. From these facts, for which it is indebted to the intelligence and enterprise of the people of Michigan, and to the faithful and energetic labors of its late President, the Rev. Dr. H. P. Tappan, the University has been enabled to increase its Buildings, to enlarge its Libraries, its Museums, its Apparatus, to call a greater number of learned men into the Faculty of the College of Science, Literature and the Arts, to establish and furnish what may, without boasting, be pronounced one of the best Medical colleges in the United States, and to endow a Law School, which, though young, already rivals the older colleges in comeliness and influence, and to-day, for the first time, is to be provided with a building adequate to its growing majesty and strength.

But astonishing as this is, the University has no more than

kept pace with the State in growth and influence. The people of this State do not deserve the flattering compliment that they have outstripped their ability or duty in attention to education. In 1845, when this University was but four years old, and already a respectable college, graduating its first class of well-trained young men, this State was to a great extent an unbroken wilderness. Over a large part of it the wolves still howled, scarcely disturbed by the pioneer hunter. Its productive wealth, the result of labor, aside from the nominal value of its unimproved lands, was probably not more than a third of what it is now. Now railways cross its territory and connect with each other; its streams are noisy with the mill and factory; its prairies are covered with wheat; flocks of sheep take the place of the wolves; beautiful dwellings have displaced the log cottages of the hardy pioneers; spires, pointing heavenward, indicate the faith and hope of the people, and that glorious galaxy into which its star was admitted only in 1837, being now threatened by the murky clouds of treason and rebellion, Michigan has sent forth her thirty thousand volunteers, and stands ready to send out as many more, among whom are seen a large proportion of the graduates of the University, ready to go where the strife is hottest, and to deal the heaviest blows for "Liberty and Union, now and forever, one and inseparable." Behold what a few years have accomplished! The desert place has become a garden, the wilderness blossoms as the rose. Can it be possible that a University belonging to such a people will not prosper? Is not its fame linked with the State whose name it bears? Will it not

Grow with its growth and strengthen with its strength?

Universities in some form exist in all Christian countries. They are the highest institutions of learning in those countries, employing the most accomplished teachers, to whom those youth resort who are the most devoted to the cultivation of the mind. It has been flippantly denied that there are universities in America. So have I heard it reproachfully stated that America has no Church, and once it was common to assert that she had no army, and only an apology for a navy. There are those who cannot recognize an identity of character without an absolute identity of form. Though our nation has no established Church, like the Greek Church of Russia, or the National Church of England, or of Prussia, yet it requires no extraordinary powers of observation to perceive, beneath the independent and numerous denominations of Christians in this country, an unorganized unity of sentiment and action, accomplishing, perhaps more efficiently, the genuine object of a Church. So too, though our army in time of peace, and our navy, do not rival the proportions of some inferior States, yet the experience of the past two years has proved that America was not destitute of the nucleus of organization for defense equal to any of their kind in the world.

The United States of America have long had institutions of learning that might justly bear the name of universities. To that class they clearly belong, and by the proper standard of such institutions they claim to be judged. They partake, by necessity, of the character of the nation. Universities everywhere are sensitive to those complicated influences which make up the national character, and are therefore continually changing. In spite of the apparent immobility which is supposed to attach to them, they and the national character are reciprocally sensitive, and constantly act and react upon each other. Generally, with only a few extraordinary exceptions national influence and the glory of the universities rise and fall together. As the nation grows in wealth and consideration the universities increase in power, though there are instances in which abundance and luxury have lowered the standard of severe study, and poverty and disaster have impelled the ambitious to earnest intellectual labor, thus preparing the way, by one of the divine methods of compensation, for national relief and triumph. Intellectual forces and moral integrity lie at the basis of ultimate success. The universities of America are for the most part young, and are therefore inferior to some in older nations, both in useful material and useless lumber; in the powers of time-honored usages and in the embarrassment of absurd or effete forms; they are inferior in wealth but superior in enterprise; inferior in the number and experience of learned professions, but superior in their industry and effort to benefit the students; inferior in their power to secure the attendance of the students for a long term of years, but superior in their ability to crowd into a limited time the greatest amount of information and discipline. Many of these peculiarities are becoming modified with the increasing maturity of the nation, but some are permanent and others will arise.

American colleges were originally modelled after the colleges of Great Britain, inasmuch as our earliest learned men were graduates of those colleges, and naturally attempted to reproduce those modes of instruction and culture with which they were familiar. But as our government and statute and common law, though growing out of those of Great Britain, are peculiar, so the founders of American colleges soon found that there were several defects and blemishes in English universities, arising from the state of society, which they would not reproduce if they could; and time has demonstrated that there are other peculiarities in the universities of Great Britain which we could not reproduce if we would. The recognition of caste in society, even in the requirements of the colleges, and in the classification of the students; the adoption of two courses of study, the one for the studious and ambitious and the other for the lazy and feeble who, for their rank, or money, must be allowed to graduate without a thorough education—indicated by the terms "pass course" and "class course;" the system of hasty preparation for examination by the aid of private tutors; the observance of multitudinous regulations founded on the stipulations of eccentric benefactors; the foundation of fellowships the holders of which are bound to celibacy; the direct connection of the institutions with the government of the nation, giving them in some cases representation in the

National Parliament—these and many other peculiarities could no more be transferred to America than its Lords and Commons, or its clouds and skies.

On the other hand the universities of America have found that they must conform themselves to the demands of the people, and therefore greatly modify and improve old courses of study, establish new methods of discipline and of the division of labor, new penalties and rewards and new customs, thus acquiring, as all vital things have, a character of their own. Every nation must have its own peculiar institutions. All imitations are necessarily weaker than their models, while vital growths alone are strong.

I shall enter into no labored comparison of the merits of American colleges with those of other lands, only here observing, that, in vigor of growth, in nobility of purpose, in the advancement of science, in the careful attention to the moral good of their pupils, and in a healthful result upon the civilization and welfare of the people, American universities have not been surpassed by any in the world during the past half century. American colleges have principally educated our professional men and statesmen; they have been the birth-places of great moral enterprises that are shedding the light of science and religion upon this and other lands, and of thoughts embodied in books whose potency no mathematics can measure and no finite mind comprehend.

The highest institutions of learning in this country have been mostly of two classes, which for convenience I shall denominate Church colleges and State colleges. A Church college is one which is recognized as belonging to a particular denomination of Christians, with which principally or entirely its Trustees and Faculty are connected. The oldest of the American colleges were mostly of this class. Among them may be mentioned Harvard College, Unitarian, though of late the State of Massachusetts, on account of having rendered it great pecuniary aid, has assumed a co-ordinate superintendance of its management; Yale College, Trinitarian Congregational; Princeton

College, Presbyterian; Brown University, Baptist; Columbia College, Protestant Episcopal; and the Wesleyan University, Methodist Episcopal. These I mention merely as well known specimens of Church universities. In all of them and in others of this class, the course of study is as rigid and thorough as young men of fair intellectual ability and application, can complete in four years, after a prescribed course of preparatory study pursued elsewhere, while some of them have also professional schools of Law, Medicine, and Theology, and some of them have also, of late, offered the use of books, lectures, apparatus and instruction, by which investigation into some departments of science can be pursued farther than in the course of study prescribed in the undergraduate college and in the professional colleges. The great inducements to young men to enter at once into active life in this country, have, as yet, prevented a very extensive call for university instruction in advanced studies and topics remote from general practice, but as the call increases our oldest and ablest universities are preparing to respond. Courses of University Lectures are already provided for in Harvard University and in Yale University, and must be provided in a few of the largest universities in different parts of the country.

Church universities have some peculiar advantages. There is a compact and vigorous agency responsible for their character. They appeal to a clearly recognized part of the community for patronage and support. The denominations to which they belong watch over their interests, and usually harmony is easily maintained among the trustees and faculties. It would impugn history to deny that colleges of this character have accomplished and are still accomplishing incalculable good. But it is evident that there are some disadvantages inseparably connected with Church universities. An institution belonging to a particular denomination cannot possibly be so liberal and impartial as one resting upon the broad basis of the state. No efforts at impartiality, can possibly prevent, at least, an indirect preference of the party or sect on which it principally depends for character and support. This peculiarity is much stronger in some Church Colleges than in others—in some being scarcely noticeable, in others so marked as to be decidedly disagreeable to all except those who sympathize with the views and usages of the denomination owning the institution.

The second class of the highest institutions of learning, which are denominated State Universities, are of later growth, being naturally the last institutions established, or receiving any good degree of completion, as a part of the great American system of education. Whatever may have been the fact elsewhere, in this country the *primary* public schools, designed directly for all the children, received, properly, the first attention of the States, and systems of public education were devised and put into operation and largely developed, before the attention of the community was called, through their legislative bodies, to the importance of colleges or universities, as an inseparable part of a public system of education. Therefore, leading minds, of enterprise and philanthropy, were compelled to establish the first colleges without much public assistance. The legislatures would indeed incorporate their trustees, and, in a few instances, grant them pecuniary aid, but it was long before the people came to perceive and feel the necessity of completing their system of public education, by establishing normal schools and universities. In some instances the States, having aided the Church colleges, demanded some control in their government, and thus it has come to pass that several of the older Church colleges are perceptibly changing their character into State universities, and it is not improbable that many of them will yet be placed solely under the government of the representatives of all the people. There are also a few institutions called State universities, which were originally largely the product of individual benevolence, and are controlled by trustees so far removed from the influence of the people that they cannot be regarded as fair specimens of that kind of universities, which are properly called State universities, and which form a natural and necessary part of the American system of public education, when it is complete.

The University of Michigan is the oldest, largest, and most flourishing of the class of institutions that may rightly be regarded as State universities. Founded by a grant of land made by the United States, aided by grants made by the State of Michigan, recognized in the Constitution of the State, and governed, according to its provisions, by a Board of Regents, elected from time to time by the people, it is purely a STATE UNIVERSITY, entirely free from sectarian or sectional control or bias. It should therefore aim to become a model of its class. Its influence is not confined to itself, great as that influence may be. Its growth, members and power will undoubtedly cause it to be regarded either as an example or a warning to the younger States of the Union, and, in the course of time, even to the oldest States, as they successively may establish universities of this kind.

It cannot be denied that such an institution is exposed to peculiar difficulties and dangers. It may be well to examine them that we may be prepared if possible to surmount them. Allow me to suggest the two greatest, interrogatively.

Is it necessary that State universities should be irreligious? Is it a fatal necessity, growing out of their very constitution, that they should neglect the doctrines and the practices of Christianity, and by consequence have no foundation for morality? Must they be the fountains of intemperance and vice, and must the education they furnish be secular and atheistic? That this is the charge of their enemies, and the serious apprehension of some of their friends cannot be denied. But this charge, it should be observed, is not confined to State *universities*, but applies with equal force to all schools of every grade that are supported and controlled by our American States. It seems to be the conviction of some persons, mostly those who were educated in the older nations which have national churches, that a Republic, like the United States, without an established church, and granting equal protection to all religions, must be infidel, and specially do they believe, that educational institutions sustained by such a government, and on so liberal a foundation, must be irreligious, if not atheistic. Even some men in our own country, of feebler minds, or who simply echo the sentiments of their foreign theorists, with whom they have a fancied and servile connection, have repeated the same apprehensions.

The fact however is that, practically, American schools, supported by the government, are more truly religious than the average character of the people they are designed to accommodate. It is worthy of notice that the most devout and truly religious portion of educated men are the most likely to be interested in educational matters. By sympathy they are attracted to the profession of the teacher, in which the consciousness of usefulness is a greater reward than the sudden fortunes and gratifications of ambition, promised in other departments of industry.

The people too, well taught in their respective religious organizations, expect and demand that their public schools should recognize the Bible as the foundation of morality, and should inculcate in the minds of the young the great principles of Christian faith and practice. Therefore, in this country, our public schools, our normal schools, and all schools of any grade, supported by public funds or taxation, have taught morality and religion as purely and efficiently as any denominational schools whatever.

Now what has been found true in this country with regard to the primary schools, the higher public schools, and the normal schools, may and should be also true of the State universities. The average religious character of the people ought to be such, and I believe it is such, that they will and do demand, by a decisive majority, that the instruction given in their universities shall be permeated with genuine religious truth and practice. It would shock and disgust the people to learn that in their universities science was divorced from religion, or that the professors formed so strange an exception among the men devoted to teaching, as not to give proper prominence to the theoretical and practical principles of our common Christianity. Thus first, merely as an effect and not as a cause, State universities, in States where the *people* are religious, must reflect the character of the people. But they will in the second place, also rise above the average popular character, in morality and religion, from the natural tendency of religious men to the profession of teaching, and also from the fact, never to be forgotten in the consideration of democratic institutions, that the judgments of the people are always superior to their practice, so that even men who in their private character disregard the requirements of true piety demand it in those public institutions for which with others they are equally responsible. There is a sense in which the old maxim, *vox populi vox Dei* expresses a profound truth.

I maintain, therefore, that a State University in this country should be religious. It should be Christian, without being sectarian. The great and common principles of morality, received by all Christians, should be sedulously taught and scrupulously regarded, not merely as conventional rules but as principles of divine truth. The true basis of them, which is God's own word, should be recognized and honored. Those simple and central common practices of the worship of God and Christ, in which all can engage, should be regularly observed. The Holy Scriptures should be read and explained, psalms and hymns of praise should be sung, and all who resort to the University for instruction should be encouraged to adhere faithfully to the usages of that branch of the Church of Christ with which they may be connected. Especially should the bonds of union between science and revelation be shown. The professors should be men capable of perceiving and illustrating the evidences of the divine origin of Christianity, in language, mathematics, the laws of material things, and of vegetable and animal life; in history and art, and in the mind of man. The errors of the irreligious, ancient and modern, with their pernicious consequences, should be fearlessly exposed. Especially should American youth be taught that the perpetuity of our freedom depends entirely upon the integrity and genuine Christianity of the people. Those questions upon which denominations differ—however vital they may appear—should be left to their acknowledged teachers out of the University, or be so respectfully and impartially stated as not to offend the conscience of any sincere believer.

I earnestly invoke, therefore, in behalf of the religious character of this University, the sympathy and hearty co-operation of all Christians of all denominations in the State. I assure them that the University shall co-operate with them, in teaching and enforcing and illustrating Christian faith and practice; and I trust that there shall go out from its halls many hundreds of men, who, as ministers of the Gospel, lawyers and physicians and teachers, and as faithful workmen in all the industrial pursuits of life, shall, together with many of this character already among the alumni of this University, enforce and exhibit sound morality and genuine Christian culture. Let it be the object of the Faculty to show that the grand theory of American education has no fatal defect; that, on the voluntary system, Christianity may flourish and be respected, and may comfort and sustain and adorn those who embrace it, not by compulsion, but as the choicest gift of Heaven to man, through him who assures us that his kingdom is not of this world. The professors in this University must not and will not consent to be deprived of the glorious satisfaction of being co-workers with Christ, in the divinely appointed enterprise of evangelizing the world. No earthly reward could tempt them to such a compact with evil. Were their salaries to be multiplied a hundred fold, so as, instead of affording them, as now, merely a comfortable support, to give them each an independent fortune, they would not be bribed to dissociate themselves from the greatest leaders in science and culture in this and every land, who are striving to elucidate the will of God and to benefit their fellow men.

Another objection to State universities is suggested in the inquiry, Must they necessarily be political institutions? In free countries like ours the word political has acquired a limited and unworthy signification, similar to the word sectional or partisan. From some profound law of human nature it is found that in all free countries there always are two parties, nearly balanced, and frequently exchanging with each other the responsibility of holding the reins of the government. I cannot here pause to investigate whether the existence of these two parties arises from a natural contest between the conservative and the progressive elements of society, or from a natural desire for the honors and rewards of political power, or from the divine intention of a constant exchange of responsibility in government, as regular as the circulation of the blood in the living body or the great tidal waves in the ocean and air, essential to purification and life. Whatever the causes, actual or final, such parties always have existed in popular governments, and may be presumed to be an inseparable adjunct of freedom. But the vital question with us, in this connection, is, Must the State institutions of education, on this account, in free countries, be vascillating and fluctuating? Must they be continually changing their policy and character? Must their Faculties be exposed to the danger of sudden removal with the frequent transfers of political power from party to party? Must schools become a part of the spoils of office? This has been a serious apprehension of theorists, and it must be confessed too, that some facts have arisen showing that the apprehension is not altogether fanciful and theoretical.

We may arrive at the true solution of this inquiry by observing that the American States have established and are maturing a system of education, beginning with the primary school and ending with the University. All the parts are alike essential to this system. Each part must prosper to make the other parts prosper. If the primary schools are vigorous and healthy, the University will naturally be strong, but if the University suffers the primary schools will suffer.

> From all this wondrous chain whatever link you strike,
> Tenth or ten thousandth breaks the chain alike.

Now is it the will of the American people, or is it a fearful necessity of popular governments, that their educational institutions should be complicated with the fluctuations of political parties? I answer decidedly, No. Facts also answer, No. These schools, like the mountains and plains and oceans and rivers, are to be permanent, while the superficial atmospherical phenomena of political partizanship play around them. These are too essential, too sacred, to be constantly changing. By common consent these are to be cherished whatever transitions in other matters may be allowed. The American people are sufficiently enlightened and impressed with the intrinsic value of these institutions, to maintain and show to the world that no changes in opinions or in office holders shall be allowed to interfere with the primal interests of public welfare, represented in their public schools, from those in which the alphabet is taught, to that in which the last results of human investigation are made known. The primary schools, the public academies, the normal schools, and the universities, are entirely removed from the manipulations of party politics. It is only in young States, not yet skilled in self control, or disciplined by bitter experience, that the government of the university is sensitive to popular political excitements. It is an indication of immaturity, and of a want of the highest civilization, to carry party politics into educational matters; and it is a serious reproach to any State that ever the preferences of any political party should be seriously insisted upon in the choice of an officer to superintend general educational matters, or to hold a position as an instructor in any public school. No man is competent for such an office who does not, at least in all his official duties, rise above subserviency to party control or preference.

This theory is already verified in the practice of our most enlightened States. It is true of Michigan. I aver that the example of Michigan shows that a State University is not necessarily involved in partisan politics. I am not aware that any such influence has been felt in its government for many years. It may indeed be questioned whether it was ever felt, certainly not since it received from the people its present admirable system of government. It should be one of our objects to show to the younger States and to all the world, that a great university can be established and maintained and continned in action as regular as the laws of nature, without any sensitiveness whatever to those revolutions in public opinion on political matters which give rise to changes in the administration of the government of State or Nation.

But while the university rises serenely and supremely above partisan turmoil, I desire plainly to announce, that in my opinion the University of Michigan should have a decided political character. If it be a fault, nevertheless I acknowledge it as a logical and moral necessity, growing out of its origin and fundamental character. The University of Michigan is partly the gift of the United States of America to the people of this State, and partly the result of the enterprise of this State itself. For its endowment and support it is coordinately indebted to the Nation and to the State whose name it bears. It owes allegiance therefore both to Nation and State. The life-blood that flows through its veins comes from every State in the Union. Its students come from many States. It is the product of American enterprise and American thought. It is one of the exponents of the fact that the United States of America prize sound learning and thorough culture. Its history forms a striking chapter in the history of the Nation, showing that this whole people prize civilization, science, literature, thought. The University therefore owes allegiance, fidelity, and the best support it can give to the whole undivided nation. It would be unworthy and disgraceful for the University to teach, or countenance, or tolerate within its precincts, the presence of treason. It must therefore be political, in the highest and best sense. It is American. It is democratic, not aristocratic. It is republican, not monarchical. It holds to the principles which Hamilton promulgated and which Washington maintained on the field and in the Presidential chair. Its Professors must, and always will, and always can, show from nature and history and science, that the Almighty Ruler is in favor of those sublime and benign principles that finally blossom and ripen in self-government and an enjoyment of the right to life, liberty, and the pursuit of happiness. And when an emergency arises, be it from foreign despots or rebels at home, it should be found that the great body of its alumni will be ready, as now, to devote their fortunes, honors and lives to the Nation that has given them their education and power. Thank God that the University of Michigan has always been political in this noble sense.

A university in order to attain the maximum usefulness must have some primal elements of success, which it may be profitable to notice. The first of these, and most essential, is money. Nothing else can supply the place of material strength. If the love of money is a root of all evil, money itself is a root of all good. Careful observation will show that the want of property is the greatest hindrance to the full development of a university in a new country. There is not a university in the United States of America that has yet escaped the constant galling pressure of poverty. Our oldest and best endowed colleges of the Eastern States, which have received, for more than a century, donations from individuals and aid from the State, find themselves constantly prevented from accomplishing their own conceptions of what science and the best interests of the community demand, by the want of money. Our most eminent scientific men are often seen spending a large part of their time in earnestly soliciting donations to the literary and scientific schools with which they are connected. Some of them deprive themselves of nearly all the luxuries of life that they may prosecute their investigations and diffuse information. Science has ts martyrs as certainly as religion.

A university needs money to procure suitable lands, buildngs, libraries and apparatus, and to support competent instructors. Much of the material employed is perishable and needs frequent renewal. Often special investigations are desirable, requiring large sums of money, the returns for which are not to be expected in gross substance that can be measured and weighed, but in the settlement or explosion of a theory, the suggestion of a new hypothesis, demanding in its turn to be tested, or in some enlargement of the area of correct thought.

In these experiments many failures are to be expected, but the expenditure of time and money is not therefore lost. Superficial and narrow observers often complain of such an expenditure of material, and seem to think that the money employed to promote science and the highest education is wasted. They are not aware of the inconsiderableness of the amount of money thus expended, when compared with that employed for other objects, nor of the value of the profit received. They have not observed, perhaps, that the cost of building and equipping one ship of war would endow a university as liberally as the University of Michigan, and the expense of keeping a ship of war in repair and in active duty would more than supply all the demands of such a university after its endowment. The cost in money, of a single battle, would more than double the permanent resources of this University. The amount of money expended in this country on a single fourth of July, in the explosion of gunpowder and other fulminants for noise alone, would give the Nation several valuable institutions of learning. I adduce these facts not to express disapproval of ships of war, or battles, or even of the explosion of powder for noise. Man liveth not by bread alone. Man needs more than food and raiment. It is one of the shallowest conceits of feeble minds that whatever does not produce gross property is useless. We need civil law and a sound government, and if these cannot be secured without ships of war and cannon, and the paid labor of strong and educated minds and of strong and trained bodies, let the requisite demand be met, though it cost a hundred fold more than now. So too man needs amusement, the pleasures of social life, and the cultivation of the heart and mind, and though these should cost a thousand fold more of labor and money than now, the expenditure would be wisely made. Universities are one of the essentials of civilization. They are not excrescences or superfluities, but an inseparable element of a civilized Nation. No nation, state, or city yet, has ever been extravagant in their support. The maximum of good to be obtained from them has never been reached, and till that point is attained all increase of expenditure upon them, if wisely directed, is good economy, and all withholding of money from them is wasteful and impoverishing.

Looking at society as it is, with only its present degree of enlightenment, at the enormous tasks set before the people in this new world of America, and at the abundance of demagogues who are seeking power by fomenting the prejudices of the people, and by stimulating a jealousy of educated men, it is a matter to awaken profound gratitude to Almighty God, and to increase confidence in the competency of the people to secure their own best interests, that so much has been done in this country for the promotion of education. From this point of view the prospect is bright and encouraging. But when we consider that much of the educational property in this country has arisen from the sale of wild lands, and from contributions made merely for pecuniary speculation, and also in many cases through the enterprise of a few leading and noble individuals to which the great mass of the community simply assented or did not openly disapprove, but showed no hearty co-operation in these enterprises, the matter assumes a less favorable aspect. And when we reflect that the resources from wild land in this country must soon cease, and that the income from invested funds will gradually depreciate, and that whatever material increments to our educational power is hereafter made must sooner or later come from the direct and voluntary devotions of the people; it is evidently seen to be the duty of every enlightened man to impress upon all other minds, so far as he can, the fact that educational institutions, from the primary school to the university, are an essential element of civilization, and need still more of the people's power and support.

The University of Michigan has a strong and broad foundation. It cannot complain of the past. But it is yet, like the State whose names it bears, young. It would be a reproach to the State should it now cease to grow in strength and wealth. The State itself will find frequent opportunities, without an appreciable increase of its burdens, to add to the resources of the

University. Benevolent individuals in this State, will yet emulate the liberal and patriotic men and women of the older States, and leave to the University funds for the endowment of new professorships, or for the enlargement of its resources and usefulness. This element of power, I trust, in the day of need, will not long be wanting. Thankful for the past we will trust God for the future, while we strive to render the University, from its efficiency and high moral and scientific character, worthy of the liberal support of able and benevolent individuals in the community, and of the State.

I doubt not the time will come when this University shall be honored with many benefactions, and shall become a monument of individual enterprise, as well as of public patriotism and wisdom.

Another element of success in a University is a competent and efficient Government. The body of men who stand behind the Faculty, and hold the springs of the institution, can, if weak, or partisan, or malicious, ruin the university, and must in all cases be intelligent, competent and honest, to give to it a proper character. In some universities this power is a Board of Trustees elected for life and almost independent of all influences but public opinion. In some instances, in other countries, the directing power is the Government of the State and entirely independent of the people. Wisely, in this University the Board of Regents is elected by the people of the State, each Regent for eight years, and hereafter two every two years, so as to secure a constant and regular renewal of the Board, without abrupt changes, which are likely to be attended with great disasters. No genuine American should regret that the people of the State thus directly control the University. This is the true republican idea. It harmonizes with our institutions. All experience tends to prove that in such a way an enlightened and honest Board of Regents will be obtained. The people will naturally select for such an office men who have exhibited an interest in educational matters, and who from habits of thought and experience are competent to the management of so important an enterprise. At the same time if an abuse, real or fancied, arises, the public will not be slow to elect men who will remove the evil. A university thus governed will never be allowed to become a fountain of error or immorality, but will execute the purpose of the people. Whatever therefore tends to benefit the entire community will benefit the University.

At the same time through such a government healthy reforms may be easily accomplished. The new and special demands of the present times will not be disregarded, and the University will therefore not be a slavish imitation of some distant model, nor an unchanging relic of the past, but will be kept constantly in vital sympathy with the present demands of the community.

The people of this State have reason to be grateful that the Regents whom they have elected have faithfully represented the State in a profound regard for a thorough and practical education, for pure morality and genuine religion, and that they have managed the University with such successful economy in its financial interests, and with such fidelity in all the grave trusts reposed in them.

Another most essential element of success to a university is an able Faculty. Without competent instructors all other material is useless; with them, by ingenuity, genius and skill, the lack of other material can be to a great extent overcome. A Newton with an ordinary spy-glass will accomplish more than an indolent or inefficient man with the best telescope ever constructed. Nothing can be substituted for intellect, discipline and culture, which will be manifested in a ready command of material, and in a commanding influence over young and studious minds. The choicest men in their respective departments should be employed as professors in a university. Those only who have the requisite mental power, and who exhibit an aptitude for their peculiar work should be honored with such a post. The character and efficiency of the university come from them. The silent and passionless printed page can never take the place of the flashing eye and the living voice. The first and most efficient medium of conveying thought and emotion from mind to mind is by the exercise of speech, and therefore the office of a professor can never become obsolete.

The power of a university will bear an exact ratio to the number of competent men it can employ in its Faculties. As an institution increases in wealth and strength the division of labor which it will secure by the multiplication of departments, or increased subdivisions made in the boundless area of human knowledge and investigation, will enable it to accomplish more and more successfully the fundamental object of a university.

Here, however, in our American universities a great practical difficulty arises. The traditions and usages of our colleges are in favor of certain courses of study, limited in time, and therefore limited in their range of investigation. The undergraduate course, so called, taking young men at that degree of advancement in the classics and in science which they easily reach in our union schools and academies, has been limited to four years, at the expiration of which the students, if they have average capacity and have maintained proper diligence, are accounted worthy of graduation as bachelors of arts. Here the college life of many of the students has been accustomed to end. Professional colleges for those who wish to study medicine, law and theology, have been respectively connected with our ablest universities, in which also courses of study limited to two or three years have been established, at the expiration of which the students, if successful, graduate as physicians, lawyers, or clergymen. But it has been found that outside of the branches of study pursued in these respective departments or colleges, there are other subjects of investigation in which many are interested, and for the prosecution of which the university should furnish adequate material and personal aid. This demand has been met more promptly and efficiently in American universities than in the English universities, and yet much remains to be done. To supply this demand various means have been suggested, and to some extent tried. It has been proposed to force into the four years' course of study for undergraduates a greater variety of subjects, and to bring the students under the tutelage of a greater number of professors. A fatal objection to this course is the inevitable consequence that what is gained in surface is lost in depth. So simple a problem ought not to puzzle any mind. One factor in the problem—the term of four years—is limited; the capacity of the youthful mind to obtain information and discipline is also limited, and to expect any perceptible increase of result, when these factors are employed, must be fallacious. Whenever this has been tried, therefore, it has practically failed. Others have suggested that with the improvements of the times the undergraduate course of study should be amended by the rejection of certain branches which are said to be obsolete and unnecessary, and by the substitution of others more immediately and universally useful. This objection generally takes the form of undervaluing the Latin and Greek languages, and of some departments of the pure mathematics, and recommends the substitution of modern languages and the study of nature. This proposed method of relief is undoubtedly illusory and radically wrong, based as it is on a fatal want of comprehension of the real object and absolute advantage of a thorough training in Latin and Greek and the mathematics. This object is not so much practical information as practical strength; and with due respect to the opinions of a very small number of genuine scholars who may think otherwise, there is no doubt in the minds of the ablest and best scholars, that no course of study can be devised so well fitted to secure a thorough and harmonious development of the whole mind and heart, and to serve as the basis of the most thorough scholarship, as the curriculum of study which is pursued in the classical course of our colleges, and in all institutions throughout the civilized world, in which the foundations of what is called a liberal education are laid. To lay aside or to interfere with this course, except to perfect it, would be suicidal of the best interests of the university.

The end proposed, therefore, cannot be obtained by the omission of any branch.

It has been proposed by others to extend the undergraduate course of study from four to five years or more, thus giving opportunity for the multiplication of topics. To this there is the strong objection that it would make our undergraduate course different from that of other institutions in the same country, while yet it would bear the same name. It would not secure the attendance of any more students in advanced studies and would simply lessen the number that would graduate. The true question at issue is, not when a student shall *graduate*, but how shall he be aided to study all that appears desirable?

There is but one proper or practical way to meet the difficulty. As far as may be, let extra courses of study be provided for. Whenever a sufficient number of students apply for a uniform course of instruction, differing from those primarily established, let a department be created and recognized, and let the system of classification, as far as possible, be combined with the gratification of individual preferences. This is already largely done in the University of Michigan. The Scientific Department is a full four years' course of rigid study, omitting the ancient languages and substituting German and French and a thorough study of our own language. Let those who prefer this course enjoy the advantages of the University to the largest extent which they desire. The classes in Analytical Chemistry and in Civil Engineering have also opportunities to press their investigations under competent professors, and with abundant material as far as they may desire.

Provision is also made for those who wish to investigate any other department, by the appointment of competent professors who stand ready to render all needed aid.

I would respectfully suggest that a demand for the advantages of the highest university instruction, aside from and in advance of our regular course of study, must be encouraged by the university itself, before it will assume any great magnitude or intensity. The taste even for a college education is not altogether a natural instinct, but is encouraged in the community by the great body of college graduates, and by the evident rewards that follow its faithful accomplishment. By the same principle the valuable discipline and information that the university stands ready to impart, above that which has been customarily crowded, in American colleges, into the undergraduate course and the ordinary courses of professional study, must be advertised by the university. Universities must accommodate themselves to the spirit of the age, and advertise their powers. The facts must be kept before the public; and those who would qualify themselves for professorships and the higher walks of science, should be informed that in the University of Michigan, ample facilities for such an object are supplied. However few persons may apply for the advantages, they should be accommodated, it being constantly borne in mind that the higher the education furnished in any institution, the smaller will be the number of those seeking it. Our very highest classes will perhaps always be small in number. In this way our American system of education may be developed into a beauty and efficiency unrivaled, and become as clearly superior in its highest as it already is in its elementary departments.

There is no good reason why those departments of education principally attended to in what are called theological schools, should be systematically neglected in a State university. Such a neglect betrays either a wrong conception of education or a fear of opposition, calculated rather to awaken the contempt of the people, than their approval. The first organic law of the Territory of Michigan for the establishment of a university, contemplated giving due attention to such studies. The first report of the first Superintendent of Public Instruction eloquently and logically showed its necessity. The late President of the university, in his excellent Inaugural Address, delivered here nearly eleven years ago, said:

"Our institution being a State institution, and therefore connected with no particular denomination, cannot establish a Theological School on the University fund. But it is to be hoped that the different denominations will establish professorships in the different branches of theological science in this town. In some of these branches they might unite, in others they would choose to establish separate professorships."

This is certainly a valuable thought; but what is to hinder the immediate establishment of a professorship of the Hebrew language and the cognate languages, and their literature? Is there fear of offending any person whose opinion is entitled to any consideration, in the careful study of one of the primal languages of human speech, in which poets sung and orators spoke, when Greece herself was barbarous, and the seven-hilled city was an unbroken wild? If not for the sacredness of its revelations, still, for its antiquity, and for its essential value in philological investigation, it should not be neglected in a university. And what mind is so squeamish about offending prejudice or conceit as to pronounce it impossible properly to consider, in a State university, the thoughts, beliefs, and revolutions of opinion and action that constitute the basis of what is properly termed ecclesiastical history? The very foundation and frame-work of every modern nation in Europe and America have been shaped by ecclesiastical thought and action, and now to turn away from it or to neglect it, or not to give it proper attention and study, betrays a timidity that might well awaken the contempt of the truly intellectual and liberal. With the two professorships of the Hebrew Language and Ecclesiastical History, any denomination of Christians might easily, and with little expense, furnish the small additional instruction which, outside of the university provisions, they might deem necessary for those whom they intend to recognize as worthy to be teachers of the people in morality and religion. Thus the university of Michigan would fill a chasm which some have supposed inseparable from an institution founded by an American State. Thus we should be prepared to show that in no particular is it compelled to fall behind the best and most complete universities of this or other lands.

I trust that this suggestion will awaken the attention of those who most appreciate the essential value of religion as the central element of true culture. What is essential in the individual is essential in a perfect institution, and its elements and principles should be properly pursued.

Another requisite for the success of a university is a proper sympathy with it and demand for it in the community from which it receives its support. By this I do not refer to the people in the town or city where it happens to be, who are liable to be deceived about what they cannot understand, and who have no more to do with the university, on account of its being near to them, than the university has to do with their factories, or shops, or farms, or gardens; but I refer to the people of the whole State, in their constitutional relations to the university. Without their approval their university cannot fully accomplish its work. They must be taught to feel its necessity and value. To supply this demand, I appeal to the alumni, who have experienced its advantages and know its value. I appeal to those who have been heretofore honored to preside over its interests as Regents, and who have directed its great and beneficent influences. I appeal to the teachers of our public schools, reminding them of what they already appreciate, that all the public schools of the State form one system, and that the sound prosperity of a part is only to be secured by the prosperity of every other part. Especially do I appeal to the principals and teachers of our higher classes in the union schools, who are presumed, from their position, to be men of culture and liberal thought. I ask them to keep before the minds of their pupils that those whose taste or genius inclines them to it, have an opportunity freely furnished to them by the State to prosecute their inquiries into science and thought still farther, in the university, with all the facilities that the most ambitious could desire. I ask them constantly to organize and preserve classes of pupils in preparation for the university. This is clearly a part of their duty, as it is ours to do all that we can to maintain the honor and efficiency of all the public schools in the State.

Let the vulgar prejudice against knowledge be discountenanced and banished forever from an intelligent and free people. Let science continue to unlock her resources and reveal them to our gaze. Let the people continue as heretofore, through the aid of science, to rise in the scale of being and in comfort, till one by one the curses of ignorance, poverty, and feebleness are removed. Let the great forces of nature be made our obedient servants; let the experience of past ages warn us against evil and show us good; and let those engaged in the discipline and instruction of the mind, together with those employed in the spread of the Gospel of Christ, succeed in making this earth, so far as we can, an ante-chamber of Heaven, a Paradise of God.

Such, gentlemen, is my ambition. Such, I doubt not, is the purpose of all associated with me, and together responsible with me, in the management of this university. The hopes of its founders shall not perish. As its walls crumble they shall be replaced by others. Its permanency shall be that of the soul, incorruptible and eternal. It shall be the perpetual fountain of sound scholarship, genuine morality, true christianity. It shall be a glory and a bulwark of the State whose honored name it bears. That this may be the fact, may the approval and blessing of the Father of lights, from whom cometh down every good gift and every perfect gift, be upon it, not for any worth of our own, but from his sovereign mercy and for the glory of his name.

www.ingramcontent.com/pod-product-compliance
Lightning Source LLC
LaVergne TN
LVHW021201120826
845150LV00011B/2342

* 9 7 8 1 4 1 8 1 9 4 5 9 8 *